ALL THINGS DUSK

ALL THINGS DUSK

Z.G. TOMASZEWSKI

HKU
PRESS
香港大學出版社

Hong Kong University Press
The University of Hong Kong
Pokfulam Road
Hong Kong
www.hkupress.org

ISBN 978-988-8208-82-1

British Library Cataloguing-in-Publication Data
A catalogue record for this book is available from the British Library.

Epigraph in the front matter: "Trying to Pray" from *The Branch Will Not Break* © 2007 by James Wright. Reprinted with permission of Wesleyan University Press (www.wesleyan.edu/wespress).

10 9 8 7 6 5 4 3 2 1

Printed and bound by Hang Tai Printing Co., Ltd. in Hong Kong, China

CONTENTS

I.

II.

III.

This time, I have left my body behind me, crying
In its dark thorns.
Still,
There are good things in this world.
It is dusk.
It is the good darkness
Of women's hands that touch loaves.
The spirit of a tree begins to move.
I touch leaves.
I close my eyes, and think of water.

"Trying to Pray"
—James Wright

I.

The Soul

You can hear wind echo
        over water
and the loose rhythm from the well
        of the pine warbler's chest
a trill growing out
            from the trowel of its beak

You can nearly see
        the shape the song takes
            as it loops down
                    gravity-bound
        following the brook
through the sleeves of balsam fir

        freeing south—

            the source being
    carried back

You are the rambling
        sound of what fills
                a song

From silence we spill
        and silence we fall

The Composer Sheds Her Sheet Music

And opening her arms—wings fully developed—
    her eyes shift—roll—light releases—leaving behind the cocoon
        —notes escalate—she flies—
cello strings taut—the bow bends over
    the wood body—something in the composer leaps—
        the cello lifts—
the sun echoes through trees whose leaves hold dimly—
    wings of streaming water flap behind the building—
        the sheet music sweeps away with wind—
paper birds abandon their nests—the wind
    rustles the leaves of their wings—
        light fills their bones with flight—
bricks of the building crumble
    from each saw at the strings—
        the wind—the composer's hair like feathers—
clouds faded from sky—
    the building vanished—
        under our feet grass thrums—
the bow flows over water—
    cello's wood plume-stained in shades of Autumn—
        the cocoon is dust
behind us—birds spill water from their beaks—
    the sky surrounds us—
        the composer holds us—but we are the music—
we are the leaves
    and we are let go—

Day of the Dying Apples

A tree decays,
the backdrop a yellow house,
blue roof trimmed in red,
shingles slant, shambles dappled
with dew, the moss leaning toward the earth,

fermented fruits fall,
but before they smash into slaw is
the longest leap—
                    rotten and rust colored,
Seurated in an ashgray haze
with a smeared stroke of pale, exhausted brown
and on each apple a fine speck of silver—
a precise brush that captures and reflects
the slight fog of sun
squinting through smudged sky.

Two Chairs Under an Apple Tree

An old lady sits,
the fabric of her body
stitched in with the horizon.

Patches of thought cross
the sky of her mind, clouds
weave past the sun.

    Maybe the dancing
trees in the distance remind her
of her husband, how they met
in an apple orchard, their eyes
engaged—all the fruit ready for
the taking.

As the sun reels down
behind the Green Mountains,
pockets of valleys begin to fill
with fog.

    Maybe what laces
around the spinning-wheel of
her memories are his last words
to her: *Make for me a blanket big*
enough for two, so when I lay down
I can wrap the night around you.

In the chair next to her,
as the ball-of-yarn-sun
unravels out of sight, an apple,
unstrung, lands—
the world spinning
towards dusk.

Loss

You watch the yellow lace unwind
from a young girl's hair while
the mirage on the road wavers.
You replay the day your daughter
died: glittered gold streamers whirling
from handlebars as she was riding
her bicycle, totter of training wheels
tipping to keep balance,
but the hill's
                    loose gravel
and a guy driving distracted
by your wife's summer dress.
At dusk all the colors quickly
roll into the grave of night, and
come dawn they return, but one
always seems etched inside the eye.

The sun spools behind the hill, the girl
tries to secure it, but wind catches
the lace, flings it across the horizon.

Poem for Roger Allen

I stand now where you stood every evening for four decades
watching what crossed the sky as the sun set. It was the airplanes
that attracted you, but I've been here for hours and haven't
seen a jet yet. There are plenty of clouds brushing the sky over
Caspian Lake, and birds, their bodies light as clouds. I imagine
your body weighs as little. Though the first time we met: a button
on your flannel jacket busted, a broken belt-loop, a switch to
suspenders which you fetched from the back cab of your rusted
truck, and as you walked, doddering, the cousin of a whistle
snapped—most of your teeth logged off, the air curling and
unfurling to the contours of your flapping lips—maybe if a
jetstream was audible we'd hear a similar sound. And on your
face, surrounding the cleared calcium lot of your mouth,
gray hair tangled with white—a beard trailed from your chin.
Clouds ripple, in their wake an airplane echoes all things dusk.

Sound, Freckle, Cluster, Lake Light

Barn swallows breach the docks with their cursive flight,
a dance of invisible lace tying, knotting the fabric of their bodies
to the air, then, tucking their wings, unravel as a single feather
canoes through the wind.

It's when the song sweeps out and focuses on its periphery
where it draws in to the source.

There's a fence of fir trees on the north shore and the moon's
crown, tilted; a waxwing waning in its nest while gnats
gather themselves in gibbous-shaped constellations, a halo of
sound, freckle, cluster, lake light.

Summer Song of Lake Michigan

There's a billowing, boom beneath the wharf.
   Waves are singers in the wings of water,
      flapping a splashing sonata of wet feathers.

Light shines like an echo of a loon
   across the lake, colors the reflection of syllables,
      rippling in unity with wind.

Choir of cattails reaches out,
   creeps a capered chorus,
      hiss of wind,
         raspy hymn.

Boy stands regal as a bird
   in the whispering ripples:
      perched on two legs, toes as talons,
         puffed chest, back arched, elbows bent,
            wings unhinged,
               armed—in the shadows

the self is still;
   a soft symphony slips
      from his parted lips:
         a lure. Who wouldn't surrender
      to this quiet sound? Who could resist
   the temptation of centering oneself?

Song sweeps along the shore,
    slow whistle washing the body of sky-blue
      with warm hues of lake light.

The shy music of summer stirs
    and then settles
      under a sun.

Yesterday's Tide

The tide arched over
    in folds cresting upon itself
carrying on its back the body
    of a young boy—

childhood returning to me in waves—
    the strain of years on a body—
sand withered at shore—

    I'm digging with shovel-hands
where the boy washed in

    and find the farmhouse where I grew up—
white panels with evergreen
    shudders, the spruce my dad planted
to outline the property,

    the garden's plump tomatoes
with the caterpillars I would play with,
    but it was the raspberries that brought me in
to soldier its vines dodging bayonets
    for the medals I was so eager to obtain
and gaining the glory of bloodstain;

    there was my brother beside me as we crawled
with modest harvest to the road
    where we offered them to passersby;

we climbed the high oak on Ivanrest,
        branches jostled sending down twigs
and a few fragile leaves;

        it was my brother and I waiting perched
for the massive yellow caterpillar to haul us
        to our elementary school, the school like a caterpillar
compiled of brick with an arch
        as if reaching for a leaf;

there were maps and blackboards and desks'
        empty metal stomachs hungry for our supplies:
pencils erasers folders paper candy love notes:
        all of it consumed; the video in science class
about how pelicans feed in a group forming a "U"
        beating their wings against the surface to direct fish
towards shallow water where they're scooped up into accordion bills;

        our science teacher Mr. Kelley, paunchy stomach
widow's peak thick oval glasses, who hid things
        in old camera film containers
that he'd poked holes in and set around the room
        for us to identify the item within by smell:

salt and black pepper, field grass and dirt, one empty and in one
        there was cinnamon; back at the farmhouse
my mother hung cinnamon stalks to dry, how they'd curl in
        from the edges like a scroll of birch bark and permeate
the house with a warmth that practically Winter-proofed it;

my mother whose hands saved an abandoned rabbit,
milk splashed into a tiny bottle, the nib held to the bunny
who accepted before releasing it back to the wild—

so I've revived the boy
and wade with him deep into the water
past the shallows where small fish congregate
to where the tide pulls forward.

Lessen

Evening. Eating ice cream.
    At the bottom of the bowl
        probably a penny

or, if lucky, beneath two scoops
    of Superman or Bluemoon:
        a quarter.

My brother and I sat side by side
    with two years between us.
        Children. It was impossible

to know what awaited us.
    We learned not to eat too quickly
        because stomach-ache

so we allowed time to melt,
    anticipating our profit.
        Sometimes there was no money.

It was our step dad who did this, who placed
    coins (or not) under our ice cream.
        My brother saved his.

Now I sit sinking
    into the steady slurrr of
        the Grand River, no money in my pocket

but breadcrumbs and a few sunflower
　　seeds which I pitch to the birds and
　　　carry on down the waterway

a morsel or two lighter.
　　But brother
　　　where are you?

"A Gypsy Baby"

engraved on an old tombstone in Walden, Vermont

The trees turn their leaves thousand-color Autumn, clapping
    against wind.
A few have fallen at my feet, beginning to brown.
Wind flips and furls burnished red/orange leaves that curl,
    I kick, turn, and twist and suddenly see a young gypsy
    in the mirage of swirling leaves.

I let myself lift for a moment like a branch in the harsh breeze
    and notice the tree with its cloud-bruised branches
    and thunder-torn trunk.
Above us is a sky all accepting yet unforgiving with its thick beads of
    mist.
The far field of the sky breaks open, a few bits of rain become of it.
    Later it clears.
There are leaves sweeping across the tombstone and soon
    it will begin to radiate.

Now, when I walk, kicking leaves, I think of the child: no name, though
    I want to give it one, a necklace of wildflowers around its burial
    plot, a mess of beads, one weather-chewed pencil, and that voice:
the wind rattling the crisp, stubborn oakgloves, the zephyr that coaxed
the clouds in and then whispered them away, the sky that would fold and
    unfolded—not the flood, but that dance:
how we turned the soil together.

Bat

I am attracted
to the dark force
of life's other side:
the place
under a bat's wing,
that shadowed wind,
the dusk holster.

I don't know much
about that night-
indulging species, but
I see its pull
towards darkness,
its magnetic content
with the deep
sonar-burning black
track of dusk.

First Evening, Mooselung Pond

A whisper slicks from the pond's shoreline,
    creeps a visible sigh over water.

What's it trying to say, this scent
    of milkweed, daisy, black-eyed susan,
        the surrender of spruce?

What's it saying, the whisper that wakes
    the owl?
                As a boy
        I'd wake early, watch the fog
           crawl, furl, witness it shift
               under the morning light's weight.

I'd hold my breath
    not wanting to add to the thickness,
        wary of casting a spell.

Maybe that's what the mist means:
    learn to let go, even if an exhale
        seems a sort of spell, a spell that lingers
        like fog over water.

Becoming One of Them that
I Hear in the Evening

Morning, I pander
out among the pines,
perambulate Mooselung Pond.
There's fresh coyote scat where
a mushroom begins to prong up.
I gather the canine's tracks,
a penmanship of mud, read
where it came from,
where it went.
I try to collect
the coyote's scent while
the sun dulls.
As I digest this I am
losing part of myself.
Afternoon diminishes,
night sharpens its black blade.
Slowly I become
the coyote's howl.

Night Bard

The owl sharpens its song against the black whetstone of night
    as Hades echoes the old bard's hollowing.
It clicks through to my ears, I am trying to sleep.
I've fallen in rhythm with the chamber notes.
I am the air passing through the bird's beak,
    the transparent whetstone.
My bed is part of Dow's Crossing and the owl's talons are cinching
    on bark and furbacks. The owl is a logger of rodents.
Hades tosses up sawdust and it sticks to the dark ceiling like stars.
I am not the owl, nor am I Hades, but the sharpness,
    singing.

Not Wanting This Poem To Be About Me

I have seen waters turn black at the touch of the kingfisher's beak.

I have heard the coyotes masked by night howl before and after
the hunt.

I will not lie down in the satchel of the bear's stomach.

The great-horned owl is also an agent of the underworld.

I have felt in me for many years fear for the fish wanting
the suspended worm.

And have noticed how clouds try to cover the sun.

I wonder what the sapling reaches toward.

This poem is not about me.

Bear

No more does it wander rash through
the woods, but begins to settle. It's not Spring,
she's not stirred from sleep. It's approaching
Winter and she's wrapped in her weariness,
but before she dens down
she staggers south to the stream where
she sheds something of herself,
swaying with the wind, that black body
of hair swimming.

Above her
snow begins to paddle,
the first flakes of the season
shifting.

II.

Flesh and Blood

Trees and buildings become islands
in the morning mist, the valley
a strand of clouds like a scarf frayed at its edges.

When I return to the house I search a closet
for the doeskin mittens my grandfather made
from the first deer he hunted,
instead find the cap my grandmother knitted
and a felt shawl she'd sewn, and hang them on a nail
near the door—a nail found in an old maple, the one
from which sweetness used to run,
removed and brought inside after many years retired.
It was the nail on which he hung his rifle.

I imagine the deer: hooves clomping
through the woods, no fear so near to death—
death: the unknown forest.
And I consider my grandfather,
cold and hungry, quiet, waiting.
I think of the fog that must have surrounded them,
each an island in their own existence
brought together by something small and fast—
a nail to the heart.

I think to check by the wood furnace
and there, under a cloud of cinder, the mittens lay.
I steal them up, dust the soot off,
clap them against the house's exterior
sending woodash to swirl like snow.

Running Naked

I leave clothes at Milkweed Manor
open the door
dash out to Mooselung Pond:

stars fall shaped like snow,
the wet light impresses skin
like dimples. Back and forth

between my legs the hammock
of a crescent moon hangs,
sways, the silver stroke
slaps the landscape of inner thighs

and smoothes the pitched paint
of a heaven falling apart.
Underfoot tall grass bends,

the green strings
of a grounded instrument
with millions of silver bows of snow

sawing over.
Mud clumps between toes, bass-line
struck with every footfall, the heart

chanting inside the chest.
I approach the shore
as though on crater's edge

and kneel, arch spine
until on four and crawl out
breaking the shell of water—

from knuckles curl forth fingers,
between them webs extend, I tangle
in cattails and snakegrass,

catching the body in emerald webbing,
motion skyward, hands arcing
round the celestial curtain,

clench and pull down, revealing
a glimpse of light while being
enrobed in a comet's cloak.

If I Last the Night

Ceremonial dawn
docks upon the porch
and you are by the door
in a shadow waiting
until the compass in me needles
to the altar of my waking.
You will step into the light
as sun shakes dust from
the rug of the sky
while mist rises from hay
and speak to me words I know
but am not prepared for—
having become
married to something
oracular.

A Fable

Every evening as the sun sets—its gold drawn down
behind mountains—and moonlight meanders
from the east, silver shines over, into, and through
the trees, brought on the owl's back: a metallic
shimmer woven with the ripples in the pond, rolling
to shore. Bordering the shores are blue spruce and
balsam fir, conifers where fairies romp
on the tips of evergreen needles. Only when
a full moon casts a glance on the land they dance.
The trees, those stout old ladies, lift
their balsam blouses shyly during the nightstir.
Skipping out from under the plump-bottom pines
gnomes begin to gather tree-needles shed from the
spruce-sleeves where fairies carry themselves in fun.
With the needles the gnomes collect they construct
a canoe. All the while adults asleep and children dream
such things. It takes all night, but the gnomes finish
a small boat. When the sun eventually rises
they will float off, disappearing in the bright light.
And the fairies, well, they find those dreaming
children just as they begin to wake and lightly
land on their lashes; young eyes beginning to open.

Morning

In a hammock of gossamer
   silked between two stalks
of milkweed that have yet to open
   sits a spider:
she is the sun and the tangled
   insects are planets—
the spider circles them.

   Dawn blinks sending gold threads
glimmering on the silver web—
   the spider's orbit stalls—
she absorbs the light
   before rising and beginning
to cast off the small sac of moons—
   spinning another galaxy.

Dow's Crossing

The cattle pass beneath the old train tracks and I am called
down. I descend the steep slope placing left hand on aspen,
set foot, then right hand to rest against a birch branch,
lift again and set the other foot, repeated several paces,
back arched, leaning to an imaginary post
parallel to the slant of the soil, boots grip and tear
stitches of grass, dirt chucks and crumbles, tumbling
before me to the faint clearing. After slashing through yew—
wrists with bracelets of rashes—I reach the base,
an old stone foundation. A rail of light ignites the tunnel
from the other side. White stalactites from the stone ceiling hang—
a slurrr, a long, slow whisper. The hedgerows overgrown
on the railroad bend under the weight of their own length, droop
down over a section of the opening at the other end.
I shuffle forward into whatever these flowers are
that grow in darkness. I pull the carriage of my body onward
through the dank passage, closer to where there's light,
new land, but soon I pause, station still at the center. This is the bridge
that linked two towns together, the clink of Pullman carts
carrying passengers from a place they've known as their past
in the direction of a day they have yet to meet.
This bridge is where cattle followed
their instincts, their appetites, to a lambent land that held for them
an unknown promise. What is certain of the spirit but
its unsettled nature? This is the pinnacle—

the place in one's life when their pulse pitches, shifts,
clumbers and clatters like a train cart pressing on;
this is the point where hearts are held in firm anticipation, the body
approaches the opening, the eyes and mind fill with light.

Noon by Mooselung Pond

Flycatchers fetch crickets and cedar waxwings
    acrobatic their bodies, shimmering
        scales of waterskin striking them strange—

the pond is a fish swimming in place.
    Mirror of water smudged with cloudbrush,
        blackberry-sky stained white.

What was one merganser is three,
    bodies trailing the rusted compass of their slender sawbills.
        Cattails collected on the western shore—

nearby a muskrat gathers goldenclub,
    the last Summer harvest.
        Water surface quivers at the bear's slappering,

head held under fishing, she bobs up,
    in her hooked jaw a trout begins to brown.
        First leaf of a sugar maple releases,

slides a red-heavy blink on the day's blue iris.
    The rest remains deep-Summer green.
        Autumn's magic hand hard at work.

Butterfly Bush

It couldn't have been because idleness
I picked this: short stalk from a butterfly bush.
And anyway, why not be idle?
Detached from the root I sense
its pulse slow, trying to save itself—
a soft song slip from
purple-petaled tiny trumpets,
lyrics spill out of
lush gramophone limbs, sweet
fragrant flowers, violet-colored tongues
touching the once-rising sun.
Now it is setting, my fingers
fiddle upon the form—monarch
feeds musically—feeling
the delicate, the dying.
Wherever there's death: the drums
drumming life, filling the heartbeat
of something else, something not so distant.
With this wilting maybe it will make you wonder
how a butterfly confusedly comes
to the beauty that beholds the bush,
the flowers from which it desires its fill.

Heron

The old fisher-
man balances
himself against
the wind on one
leg, the other
folded, tucked
to his torso;
with a pole he
fishes—its beak
shovels at sand,
digging, water
wells up and lug-
worms lured in:
the trowel of
his bill filled.

Salad of Sorts

Okay, I'll admit when I first saw what I thought was moose scat
I hunched to feel whether crisp or soggy (crisp, baked) and curious
to hear it crunch I plucked a morsel—there were leaves encasing
palmetto berries and the grit of grinding twig skin—the color of
sunset at Caspian Lake on my palate. A dominant bitterness
sharpened with a needle of balsam fir, the scat-snack leaving
my mouth pine-dry and putrid.

Somewhere a grumbling widow
steps out onto her porch for a paper that hasn't yet arrived.

                              Turns out it wasn't moose, but
the droppings of a bear. Turns out blackberries are better
taken from the vine.

The widow sweeps sunset from her porch steps.

Dragonfly of Milkweed Manor

It flew in through the open door—
   its body a blue flame—
      leaving behind a whirling trail of smoke.

Who knows how long it was there,
   inside the cabin, the wicks of its wings
      flicking little fires.

It's not that I was worried
   the building would burn,
      I was concerned for the fly,

aware that if it remained indoors
   it'd lose oxygen and its light
      would extinguish.

So I snatched the first item at hand,
   something to usher it out with:
      a teapot—

in a quick scoop I stationed the empty kettle
   under the sky of the dragonfly's wings,
      slowly piloting the warm body from a window,

the matchstick of its tail flickering.
   When the wax from its feet thawed from glass
      I jarred the kettle upward

and placing my cold hand over top
    began to warm her. Side-stepping
        to the doorway I extended

arms, lifted the flap of hand:
    out from the candleholder the dragonfly
        torched, the ember of her body flashing wild.

Dead Deer

I stand over the rot-kissing carcass holding
in my heart this helplessness—hooves unhurried

and hopeless, white tail like a fallen flag.
I touch her muzzle, the clamped jaw
missing its soft sweep of breath.   .

I hold in my eyes its hardening brown hide.
Copper shimmers through fields of clouds.

Her stomach still swollen: a cumulus cloud
pregnant with death.
Their sleeping body becoming
weeds on the roadside.

I place my fingers upon her fur and
want to remember it all: waiting
in the decay while bugs bite at life—
wondering how they carry the deer, wondering,
if they're willing to show me, how to fly—

and vehicles screaking past, a raven staining the sky,
the sun coming to an end.

Garlic Harvest

Each time I smell garlic it's July, 2009.
I'm in Austria under a slate sky.
Isolde stands three rows west,
her humming mixes with the thrum
of the swelling beneath the soil.
All our bodies layered
with a film of dirt.

I am planted in a kitchen far
from that spice-dusted field,
brought back by the heat
as I ladle palms together and scoop garlic
from the bulb-stained chopboard,

the white petals falling.

Sky darkens, the flame
on the stove burns brighter.
Summer quickens to a boil
then begins its long simmer.

My Grandfather Chopping Wood

He never says a word.
You must know how to stack.
If wrong he will not tell you
but fix it tomorrow
when you are not around.

Many years removed
I'm working with a friend
when he asks how
one should place the wood.

Embarrassed I have forgotten
I admit I cannot recall
but throw in my memory
of the axe in his hands,
how sixty years of holding
the handle had grooved
the wood to his palm's grip—
how gravity eventually
brings all things down.

I see the axe blade
part the oak, but
before it does
rings of light focus in
my grandfather's eyes,
a concentration framed
in his glasses,
then the split.

Pinecone

        I want to hold the seeds of many
trees in my palm, I want the wind to
        lick my hands clean, carry
the forest to the floor. Just as much, I want
        to climb the pines, use my hands to
pulse its trunk, vault my bear self skyward,
        fingers skip from branch to
branch. I want to be the pinecone
        whisking the wind as I fall from the
shaking,
        but I'm not a pinecone, and soon
I will descend and when I do
        I'll need heat for my house, so I'll chop
down the tree I climbed
        hoping that from the seeds spread
there'll be a thriving tree trembling
        as another child shakes and clambers
the bristled branches.   .

Silencing the Crickets

I take the scythe, sharpen its blade.
I step out of the barn, sun's covered by clouds.
Approaching the tall grass I notice my boots untied,
I bend down to lace them.

III.

Farmland

I look west toward the pasture
   where green knuckles of grass roll
     into fingers of wheat,

oatgrass like hair flows through
   the bordering field; I see cattle
     pull stitches of sward—

the heavy jaws drawing down
   their necks, backs bowed: udders
     underneath heavy with milk.

What is this sudden thirst that
   possesses me? Not for the white
     cream, but the nipples.

Drinking Mead with John, Bowen, and Evan

We stand around the chicken coop passing
the unlabeled glass bottle from one sod-grimy
hand to another. John watches a hen as Bowen
recalls the Hardwick Memorial Day Parade of 1996:
old men wearing popcorn-bucket hats driving
three-wheelers in drunken pattern; floats rolling by
with people throwing candy to the curb
Who has any idea what they were pitching?
and the marching band that lagged a quarter-mile
behind, that could've used help from a vehicle
Maybe they should've been on a float to begin with
while they chased after the last truck
shouting through their instruments as they went.
This is when they met, John and Bowen. Evan edges
near the lone chick, distancing himself from
the conversation, but before long re-enters the group
to take another pull—
  "Where's it from, the mead?"
  "Fell off the back of a truck" John says.

Yellow-Bellied Sapsucker

Tapering needle-nose of sapsucker
spindles into a tree to feed,
a hole the circumference
of the pencil I hold, standing
in the tall grass under the birch,
white skin shimmering
in the sun that rises steady.
Up from the roots, slow
through fibers, sugar pulses
in response to the tapping bird's
hard tongue. You inch forward
toeing the flowering milkweed,
extend your neck to catch
sight of him at work. There
must be a tight spring at the back
of its head you think as the hammer-
ing continues. A few drills
and the sap begins, shy at first,
but soon spills out enough
for two. The bird bellies its share
and proceeds, leaving
a crown around the trunk—
the cornice of notches you approach,
sun at your front, black back,
lips poised ready to siphon.

The Poet in the Pinewoods

Into the spruce he steps through
air sharpened by pine needles

where creek-side sparrows join
him clutching queen anne's lace

in their small claws. The sun peels
clouds spilling thick mead

into this artery of earth where
the drunk poet's heart fills with

sweetness—the sky's fruit hanging
ready for harvest. The poet plucks

a word or two, winds them in
his mind then releases them back

into the brimming cup of Bacchus
whistling with crickets as he walks.

Correction

I saw you and thought:
'Why not bring beauty close?'

So I stuttered,
my tongue a tin hammer, pulse pounding—and asked
if you'd 'Accompany tea.'

I meant, 'Would you care to accompany me for tea?'
How bumbling I was, like the boy in grade school

whose inner chrysalis couldn't contain such jittery wings.
I was a rusty nail,
not much for shining,

but you, those eyes:
blue of sky as Winter releases

and warmth regains; blue, too,
of the transition between Summer and Autumn—
sky-stretched smile over Stannard Mountain—

your eyes cadenced with spring waters
brushed by the wind's thousand thin fingers.

I write with the weather in my pen,
I always have.
Nib-tip like a small stone

carried on an inky stream. The ink
is black to show the light-curves from your tresses.

Maybe this will be more graceful than our meeting,
since I hadn't spoken with the fluidity of rain
as I would've liked,

how *now* the wind calms me.
I just could not bring my breath to rhythm—

the hammer of my heart trumping coherent thought.
So here's me nailing a few words together,
trying to make them shine.

A Storm Divided

Forenoon in Walden I saunter the scattered
    rows of balsam fir
as light shatters the lingering mist and
the blue spruce release their sugared spice.

Dew climbs stalks of sweetgrass,
    clings a silvery clutch
that's rounded by the sun's reflective gold touch,
wet-beads collected in the tangled stems of my leg-hairs.

    The first song of morn comes riding
the wind's back from two chickadees in black and white.
They were singing of the present—
as was I, walking on
    under the clouds beginning to form.

Still Life Broken By Rain

I praised the rain when it entered,
as the sky divided,
glimpsing movement as the light

holding the sky together undressed—
each star a button keeping the cloth

of our cosmos in order.
I said, Rain, I am grateful for
your netted display, how you shape

and reflect so tenderly, how the pond
under your spell quivers and transforms.

No longer a still life the canvas
wakes and just at that moment when
all was broken—

a heron, blue and great
carrying the fishy rain in her beak

monks ashore and transcends.

Meditation

I listen to rain as I watch tea
dripping from strainer,
drop drop,
drop,

drop.

In each splash
I imagine a Mozart, not composing
but a young boy
swimming,
hands liberated from the chaos
of conducting, arms as oars,
fingers as fish, fingerprints like gills
letting in oxygen.

Minnows

wrap the silvered leaves
    of their bodies around my legs—

a bracelet of biting swimbodies, the fish
    that, on their surftops reflect
        underside of water and sky,

nibble at dead skin surfacing
    from my shins.
        I hoist toes from the muck and feel

the crown of their lips pull away—
    an argent flash of lightning—
        a cloud of mud billows.

Kingfisher of Mooselung Pond

To wet the dry rattle in its mouth
   it plunges into the pond
      from the dead red cedar.

Lifting from a quick swim
   it returns to the gray branch
      quelched.

The branch breaks—it looks like a stone
   set there has fallen, it's the kingfisher
      who casts himself into the water—

     kahplue.

Rising once more,
   he circumnavigates
      the shore, finds another perch

to place his body.
   When he casts yet again his beak hooks
      the silvery leaf of a fish.

The creak of his throaty call
   allays as the minnow tumbles into stomach,
      silencing hunger.

Blackberry

Purple thimble body,
colors sewn
from midnight to dawn,
all dimple and cheek,
brown stubble needling out;
hanging here, late August,
knit by the sun's spinning-wheel,
plump, little sponge
weaving the fabric of water;
I sheer the green thread
of your stem, you unravel
from the tangles of vine,
spool into hand;
as I turn from the bush I see,
like a knotted ball of black yarn,
the bear at a distance,
her body, thankfully,
stitched to sleep—
full from the facts
of this fruitful earth.

Summer Afternoon

Perched on a birch
hummingbird holds repose

in the stalled clutches of its green wings.
The bird's undercarriage

heaves white,
paint scraped against bark.

There's something in this world
that slows us

no matter who you are.
Say, for example,

the scarlet stop sign
of the poisonberries

or the deflated tires
of your lungs

exhausted from running
or the idle engine

of the oil-hot sun
    weighing a heavy brake

on the vessel of the body,
    the vehicle that is this earth.

Big Bang as Seen on a Chrysanthemum Stone

Every morning I'm waked with a stamp from the sun's thumb,
push out from under a sheet and float to the window, weightless
still from night's absorbing scheme, where I look out: eyes
drift with the mist whispering through pines, the ghost voices
from sleep scattering. The wind carries its song through the
bird's throat as I see the last wick of a nightstar extinguish
when the sun finds the surface of the lake and rakes it with
the comb in its gold hand. After the daystar places a crown on
Bare Knee Hill I turn from the window where, weighed down,
I sit gathering stones of thought. Before me a single grounding
stone: chrysanthemums flowing like water with white and
gray splashes of cloud-light: A flowering motif that suggests a
moment preserved during the Big Bang, the ordering of this
universe, fairies of blossoms exploding out from an abyss of
black, minerals surfacing from the deep nothingness. And on
the revealing rock (no larger than a black cherry)—the stone
of self-control, stone of mastery over distraction—I notice the
sun's reflective fingernail as I rotate it in correspondence to the
patterns of a day; this being morning I am steadfast gathering
myself from a dream. I begin to warm, standing in a fraction of
light. I have no ambition to turn the stone again tonight.

Argument

Stalk of snakegrass in the water swims, serpentines
    with waves to another shore.
A boy stirs his feet sending ripples
    to carry it towards a thicket of cattails.
The grass coils. Slithering
      his tongue the boy insults the snake's mute rattle,
        the water hisses back.

Mooselung Pond, Sunset: Autumn's Arrival

Blue spruce and balsam fir on the northeast shore
wear an auburn crown: golds and ambers echoing
across the trees' sharp plumage.

Moss patches the stone shaped like a moose's lung,
a bronze breath—the whisper that crawls out the meadow

of wildflowers from the west.
Silvery-white quaking aspen skin, birch trunks
the color of burnt butter, and the peachy cream of clouds.

The water, trembling from a leaf deposit,
shakes itself in ruby and copper.

Birch

The birch tree beside me flakes away
bark, shedding scabs of words.

Under it, smooth wintercloud-white
and beneath that something
more pure than idea.

There's a poem in there,
whether of sunlight
running through the fibers
or the rhythm of water
as it trembles
from leaves to roots.

The death that encloses
now falls away.

Again, My Grandfather Chops Wood

I want to bring those days back, whole,
not hacked away by age,

to hear the wind moved by the blade—
the *clawk thunk crunch* of the axe swung from
my grandfather's hands, splinters of time
surfacing from the trunk, his shoulders shrugged
steadying the next section to chop, the cleaver
outlining the tree's wood body—
                              to feel slivers
in my hands from knowing how to stack.

Grandfather whispers something from his bones,
a dust I do not yet understand.

Looking Out the Window with a Spider Web

and thinking: how when threatened
the distances close in.

The silver-silked web flaps like a broken banner in wind.
At the center, its founder: the cleave spider.
Decorating the flag, wings of mosquitoes wave surrender.

Look beyond, see a country
where shopping malls replace marshes,
farmland's trammeled for churches;
a bulldozer rears a metal bucket at an oak,
one with an old treehouse in it. Why?
To widen the road
in anticipation of traffic the mall will attract.

I feel the distances close in.

Those children of the treehouse have since departed.
Sure enough, the swamp drained for a shopping center.
Their childhood memories uprooted and jaded.

And I wonder who the spider is exactly.
Trying to navigate this: a torn web.

Destination

Salt pits, sand hills, gypsum mines,
a gravel road scattered along a stretch
of the Grand River. Driving
behind a truck I was
watching a bird ride the wind,
sweeping like sand in the opening
between berms when it caught
an air tide, swirled, then was stolen:
a windshield death-kiss—
a semi-truck that scraped on without
a blink or a brake, but the bird—
the swallow, low-swinger, singer, wings so
quick—now stiffening towards dusk.
Up through the dirt and gravel
feathers cloud my view as I continue to drive.

Manifest

How does the hummingbird live its life?
With speed and sweetness.

The cow?
Gradually and with grass.

Do I dare ask the mountain
or the river that wends around it?

I want for my life the stillness of stone.
The fluidity and elasticity of water.

I want to pinch light from a darkness.
I want that darkness too.

The cow comes muscling down the path.
The hummingbird hovers above a flower.

The river whose voice is strings that hum near
my ears is forever where it is and elsewhere.

What am I hungry for?
Another spirit to bring our bodies closer.

When I'm thirsty sometimes I snatch a cloud
wring it and catch the moisture in my mouth.

I fold it in my pocket then close my eyes.
Hummingbirds hop along the ground eating grass

cattle climb trees for the nectar of berries
there's a mountain of water and river of rock.

We speak of desire as if a choreographed dance.
Stand. Shuffle. Spin spin. Step towards. Slide

away. Sway. Now steady. Surrender.
Allow your weight dissolve in the other's embrace.

There's the sun that casts its inner light outward.
There are stars close to being swallowed by darkness.

Here so many humans are asleep.
And I do not mean like a mountain.

There's a spirit separate in body
but same in source.

She was a mountain within
but has awaken.

Lord let me climb closer.

Becoming an Astronaut

I build a ladder of driftwood
and plank my steps to the moon . . .
ascending the rungs of clouds
watching waves unfold
I snatch that coin and flip it once,
twice, feeling the moon's ridges
between my mapping fingers—the light
spins and spins, sweeping
a silver-lemon breath across
the blackberry water. Up here
I'm becoming grove: an orchard
of stars, a milky fog of constellations;
a glint of light splits my next step and
I see each movement of time is
really the bending of shapes and colors.
Higher, I'm climbing—
the riverine sky, its silky current of fish.
Angling, another rung. Angling.
How is it we come to find
ourselves—in this misty leap, this
silence after a foghorn?

When the ladder falls into a pile
below me, I know.
The moon on the lake is a pyre.
And I am ready.

Sleep

Frost descends.
We are close.

A voice like dusk echoes
    over water.

Wind with the last word.

NOTES

"The Composer Shèds Her Sheet Music" is, in part, a response to Patricia Fargnoli's poem "The Composer Says This Is How We Should Live Our Lives," from her marvelous book *Necessary Light*. Read it.

Hades, as mentioned in "Night Bard," is the lord of the dead, according to Greek mythology. Because Hades is the lord of the dead he is also the ruler of the underworld and therefore is considered the "richest of gods." Sophocles wrote, "The gloomy Hades enriches himself with our sighs and tears."

"Garlic Harvest" was written after the poem "Lava Soap" by David Allan Evans.

Bacchus, as mentioned in "The Poet in the Pinewoods," is another name for Dionysus, the Greek and Roman god of the grape harvest, reputed for his intoxicated nature, and is associated with the condition of ecstasy.

ACKNOWLEDGEMENTS

Poems in this book premiered in the pages of the following:

Architrave Press: "The Soul"

Avocet: "Bear," "Body of Birch," and "Morning Meditation"

Balloons Literary Journal: "Argument"

Carbon Culture Review: "Looking Out the Window with a Spider Web"

The Citron Review: "Kingfisher of Mooselung Pond"

Cold Mountain Review: "Yellow-Bellied Sapsucker"

Fogged Clarity: "Loss"

I-70 Review: "Dow's Crossing"

Lalitamba: "Summer Afternoon"

The MacGuffin: "The Composer Sheds Her Sheet Music"

The Meadow: "Two Chairs Under an Apple Tree"

Muse: "Summer Song of Lake Michigan"

Parabola: "First Evening, Mooselung Pond," "Dragonfly of Milkweed Manor," "Garlic Harvest," "My Grandfather Chopping Wood," and "Manifest"

Scintilla: "Becoming One of Them that I Hear in the Evening"

Southword Journal: "Butterfly Bush"

Talking River: "Poem for Roger Allen"

Three-Legged Stool (The Clare Champion): "Heron"

Through the 3rd Eye: "Pinecone"

"Summer Song of Lake Michigan" was awarded second place in *The Michigan Poet*'s ekphrastic contest for which it appeared as a broadside. Tip of the cap to Foster Neill.

Great, relentless thanks to Li-Young Lee for selecting this book for publication. I must weave you a nest for the doves of your life.

I am forever grateful for Donald Hall and your
suggestions on many of these poems as they appeared
in earlier versions. Even more, thanks for the letters and
poems. They are the gift of birds.

My outstanding gratitude: Patricia Clark, Robert
Haight, Russell Thorburn, and Josh Weston. My hat
is off—thanks for having read this manuscript during
its fledgling stages and given a propitious wind for its
revisions.

A flock of thanks to Jack Ridl and Patricia Fargnoli.
Also, Chris Dombrowski, Robert Fanning, John Rybicki,
Rodney Torreson, and Judith Minty, for the readership
and strong words to build feathers by.

And to Roni Devlin: I am throwing pink balloons in the
air and waving frantically for them to fly—*thank you
thank you thank you.*

ABOUT THE HKU INTERNATIONAL POETRY PRIZE

The HKU International Poetry Prize, initiated by the School of English at the University of Hong Kong in 2010, is an international award recognizing outstanding poetry written in English. Judged by renowned poets, it celebrates a body of original work in a first book of poems published by Hong Kong University Press. The HKU International Poetry Prize looks to the history of poems and honors the craft and achievement of contemporary poets. We pay special tribute this year to Ms. Aarti Hemnani, Creative Studio and HKU Black Box Theatre manager; Mr. Eric Mok, acquisitions editor at the HKU Press; and the HKU Cultural & Humanities Fund for their generous support and dedication to the HKU International Poetry Prize.

Page Richards
Chair of HKU International Poetry Prize
Associate Professor
School of English
The University of Hong Kong